40 DAYS OF LIVING GENEROUSLY

GENEROUS
TWIST

GENEROUS TWIST
40 Days of Living Generously

Written by Bob & Janet Wielenga
www.GenerousChurchProject.org

Foreword by Brad Mitchell
www.BuildYourMarriage.org

Published by Global Outreach Development, Inc, PO Box 2414, Holland, MI 49422. Global Outreach Development provides material resources, training, and coaching to help the local church generously love, give, serve, and live. Your comments and suggestions are valued. Share your Generous Twist stories online using #GenerousTwist.

For more information about Global Outreach Development, Inc., visit our website at www.GoDevelop.org

Cover and book design: La Terminal Marketing / www.laterminalmarketing.com

Library of Congress Cataloging-in-Publication Data
ISBN 978-1-5323-8343-4

Foreword by Brad Mitchell

CONTENTS

FOREWORD

One of the first words many children learn is, "mine!" From an early age we grow up wanting to keep what is ours and take what is not ours. Some of us struggle with that long into adulthood. I know I do. And because of that inner wrestling, I knew I needed to press in and work through Generous Twist.

I've known Bob and Janet Wielenga for many years. They are humble, authentic, Christ-followers who live out what is written in these pages. I knew I could trust them to biblically guide me into places that challenge me in my spiritual growth.

Generous Twist showed me places in my soul that need transformation. It revealed ways that I can grow to be more like Jesus in the way I love, give, serve and live. I'm grateful for this devotional and the way God is using it in my own life, and I think you will be too.

~Brad Mitchell
www.BuildYourMarriage.org

GENEROUS TWIST
40 Days of Living Generously

We love ice cream.

It's the perfect summertime treat. Who are we kidding? It's the perfect treat! The creamy deliciousness is hard to pass up.

Ice cream makes us think of celebrations. Growing up, Janet's family would get ice cream after playing tennis together. We've had no problem carrying on that tradition in our own family! We also celebrated the first and last days of school with ice cream. Birthday parties at our house don't always include cake but they always include ice cream. At both our son's and daughter's weddings we had an ice cream bar.

Our favorite cone is the twist. It can be a twist of chocolate and vanilla, peanut butter and chocolate or cherry and vanilla. We like it because you think you're eating one flavor and then the twist comes and you're eating another instead. It's a twist outside the traditional vanilla ice cream cone.

Generous Twist is all about twisting our perspective when it comes to generosity. Traditionally, when we think about generosity, we think about money—how much we have and how much we are willing to give away. But generosity is so much more than that.

At the Generous Church Project, we define generosity as the attitude and act of being extravagantly selfless in the way we love, give, serve and live.

Did you catch the twist? Generosity is not just about giving, it's also about how we love, serve and live.

Psalm 24:1 reads, "The earth is the Lord's, and everything in it, the world, and all who live in it."

God owns everything. As the owner of everything, God has put us in charge; we're the managers of all that He's given us: our breath, our possessions, our time, our bank accounts, our relationships, our jobs, and the earth, just to name a few. As a manager of all God has given you, you're going to take the next 40 days to give your thoughts and actions a generous twist in the way you love, give, serve, and live. Instead of focusing on your own needs, you'll be focusing on the needs of others.

And as you begin focusing on others, you'll begin to notice changes within yourself. That's the twist. You will find unexpected joy and blessings in the giving.

Generous Twist is designed to help you become more aware of opportunities God is giving you each day to live life with a twist; generously, selflessly loving, giving, serving, and living like Jesus.

We're so excited you've decided to start this journey!

~Bob and Janet

START HERE

Each devotion is designed to be read at the beginning of your day.

START WITH DAY 1

Read.

Reread the Bible passage. Spend time discovering how the passage challenges us to live generously.

Answer the questions. If you're an 'A' student like Janet please keep in mind that the questions are there to get you thinking about the passage—don't worry about trying to get an 'A" on the questions!

Spend time in prayer. If we truly want to live generous, selfless lives, it's important to pray for others as well as ourselves. We've given you specific groups to pray for each day. Your circle of influence is the circle of people around you that you connect with on a regular basis. For example, they could be your family, co-workers, cohorts, neighbors, fellow students, or church buddies.

Selfless Actions. Each day you will be given a selfless act to accomplish. You are going to have so much fun doing this! This is a key part of the 40 days. If it is truly your desire to live generously, you must put into action the things you are learning.

At the end of the day. Use the space here to journal how you met the challenge of generosity. Maybe it went incredibly well. Maybe you struggled. No matter, either way, write down what happened and how God worked in and through you.

GOD OWNS
EVERYTHING

"The earth is the Lord's, and everything in it, the world, and all who live in it." —King David

Bible Passage

"The heavens are yours, and the earth is yours; everything in the world is yours—you created it all."
Psalm 89:11 (NLT)

Questions

1. Reread the passage. Underline words and phrases that challenge us to live generously.

2. Everything is owned by God. Make a list below of all that God has generously given to you (think of people, experiences, possessions, etc).

- Julian
- health
- Kara
- Selahs
- This car

Pray For

Others - Help me share with others what I've been given.

Peace - That I would experience peace in the fact that God owns everything.

My Attitude - That I would allow God to teach me what it means to live generously. That I would not hold on tightly to things as if I actually owned them but, instead, realize that God has simply entrusted them to me.

Today's Selfless Act

Look again at the list you made of all God has given you. Acknowledge and thank God throughout the day for all He has given you.

Journal

Looking back on your day, describe how you met the challenge of generosity.

Dear god help me share with others what I've been given.

Journal

02
DAY

WE MANAGE

"He who gives what he would as readily throw away, gives without generosity; for the essence of generosity is in self-sacrifice."
—Jeremy Taylor

········ DEVOTIONAL

Bible Passage

"You are the light of the world—like a city on a hilltop that cannot be hidden. No one lights a lamp and then puts it under a basket. Instead, a lamp is placed on a stand, where it gives light to everyone in the house. In the same way, let your good deeds shine out for all to see, so that everyone will praise your heavenly Father."
Matthew 5:14-16 (NLT)

Questions

1. Reread the passage. Underline words and phrases that challenge us to live generously.

2. This Bible passage states, "let your good deeds shine out for all to see." What are some examples of "good deeds"?

 Pray For

Others - That they would see God at work in my life.

Goodness - That the Holy Spirit would fill me with goodness.

My Attitude - That I would see opportunities to do good and then do them.

 Today's Selfless Act

Accomplish a "good deed" today. Spend time with someone who needs a listening ear. Maybe take them out for coffee.

Journal

Looking back on your day, describe how you met the challenge of generosity.

Journal

03 DAY

MANAGING IS A LEARNED BEHAVIOR

"All these toys were never intended to possess my heart. My true good is in another world, and my only real treasure is Christ."
-C.S. Lewis

········ DEVOTIONAL

 Bible Passage

"What I'm trying to do here is get you to relax, not be so preoccupied with getting so you can respond to God's giving. People who don't know God and the way he works fuss over these things, but you know both God and how he works. Steep yourself in God-reality, God-initiative, God-provisions. You'll find all your everyday human concerns will be met. Don't be afraid of missing out. You're my dearest friends! The Father wants to give you the very kingdom itself.

Be generous. Give to the poor. Get yourselves a bank that can't go bankrupt, a bank in heaven far from bankrobbers, safe from embezzlers, a bank you can bank on. It's obvious, isn't it? The place where your treasure is, is the place you will most want to be, and end up being."
Luke 12:29-34 (MSG)

? **Questions**

1. Reread the passage. Underline words and phrases that challenge us to live generously.

2. Who are the generous people in your life?

Pray For

Others - That they would be open to the Gospel message.

Joy - That I might experience joy in being generous.

My Attitude - For the Holy Spirit to fill me with selflessness and a heart for others and that I would most want to serve God with all that I've been trusted with.

Today's Selfless Act

Think of someone you know who is generous. Send them an encouraging note today.

Journal

Looking back on your day, describe how you met the challenge of generosity.

Journal

A Generous Twist Story
Bonnie's Story

"I love your lamp!"
"Well you should, it once belonged to you!"
"Oh, I had forgotten!"

We all laughed because this is often the case with Bonnie. She loves to give and we have been the recipient of many of her gifts. Two love seats, artwork, dinner out, and more. She is one of those rare individuals that holds everything with open hands. She understands that God owns it all and she just manages it. And when she gives things away she gives it away completely, which is why she doesn't remember giving it to you.

If you were to ask Bonnie what her hobby is she would tell you it's people. Her calendar is full of get togethers with people. Lunch dates, dinner dates and even breakfast dates. I'm not sure she cooks at home anymore! She remembers birthdays and anniversaries and always sends a card. It seems that each time my wife and I spend time with her she gets a text or a phone call from someone because they just want to connect with her and update her on their lives. She is a true friend who listens and prays. And while she is often late to church or Bible study, it is because she took a phone call from someone who needed to talk and needed someone to pray with them.

She has a prayer calendar that is filled with people's names. On Sunday she prays for her pastor. On Monday she may pray for Bill who is going to the hospital to have some tests done. On Tuesday she is praying for a young mom and her children. On Wednesday she is praying for Mary because she has a major exam. On Thursday she is praying for Tom and his job interview. On Friday she may be praying for someone because they are receiving their cancer treatment. And on and on it goes. If we share with her that Bob is traveling to Uganda to teach pastors she always asks when so she can put it in her calendar and she will pray daily for his time there.

Bonnie is a great example of a Christ follower who generously lives, gives, and serves. The Bible says in the book of Matthew that "Wherever your treasure is, there the desires of your heart will also be." Bonnie's treasure is people, loving them as Jesus loves them.

We're challenged by this verse because we want to treasure what God treasures, but the world's treasures are very appealing sometimes. We want to live with open hands, not holding tightly to our possessions, our house, our jobs, our talents. We want to live in such a way that others will know that we believe that God owns everything and we're here to manage what He's given us. We want to give away a lamp and then forget that we've given it away since that shows we understand that it was never ours to begin with. We want God to work in and through us so that at the end of the day we can look back and see where God has prompted us to give and we have responded, "Yes, Lord!"

Oh that we might manage well and hold everything with open hands!

PURPOSEFUL
LIVING

"Never measure your generosity by what you give, but rather by what you have left." — Bishop Fulton J. Sheen

Bible Passage

"The Lord has made everything for his own purposes, even the wicked for a day of disaster."
Proverbs 16:4 (NLT)

Questions

1. Reread the passage. Underline words and phrases that challenge us to live generously.

2. Think of all God has given you. In what ways could you be more intentional about using what God has given you for His purposes?

Pray For

Others - For everyone I encounter to see the love of Jesus shining through me

Faithfulness - to live and love selflessly

My Attitude - That I would put aside my wants and desires and seek and accomplish God's purposes for my life.

Today's Selfless Act

Go through your cupboards, bookshelves, closets, etc., and find something to give away to someone you know that needs it. Make time to get it to them this week.

Journal

Looking back on your day, describe how you met the challenge of generosity.

I gave away_____

to _____and here's what happened:

Journal

05 DAY

IMITATE GOD

"Do not waste time bothering whether you 'love' your neighbor; act as if you do, and you will presently come to love him." — C.S. Lewis

Bible Passage

"Imitate God, therefore, in everything you do, because you are his dear children. Live a life filled with love, following the example of Christ. He loved us and offered himself as a sacrifice for us, a pleasing aroma to God."
Ephesians 5:1-2 (NLT)

Questions

1. Reread the passage. Underline words and phrases that challenge us to live generously.

2. What is one way you could be extravagantly selfless today?

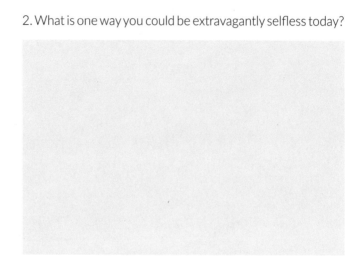

Pray For

Others - Your neighbors to see the love of Jesus shining through you.

Love - For God, family, church, neighbors, and co workers.

My Attitude - That I would be an imitator of God and live a life filled with God's love. Teach me today to love the way you love.

Today's Selfless Act

Take a homemade or store-bought baked good to a neighbor. Spend some time getting to know them.

Journal

Looking back on your day, describe how you met the challenge of generosity.

Journal

06 DAY

PEOPLE
OF LIGHT

"Earn as much as you can. Save as much as you can. Invest as much as you can. Give as much as you can." —John Wesley

········· DEVOTIONAL

 Bible Passage

"For once you were full of darkness, but now you have light from the Lord. So live as people of light! For this light within you produces only what is good and right and true. Carefully determine what pleases the Lord."
Ephesians 5:8-10 (NLT)

 Questions

1. Reread the passage. Underline words and phrases that challenge us to live generously.

2. What is one way you could extravagantly, selflessly please the Lord today?

 ## Pray For

Others - For everyone I encounter to see the love of Jesus shining through me .

Patience - Being selfless won't happen all at once, but over time.

My Attitude - May I want people to want You, Lord.

Today's Selfless Act

"I urge you, first of all, to pray for all people. Ask God to help them; intercede on their behalf, and give thanks for them. Pray this way for kings and all who are in authority so that we can live peaceful and quiet lives marked by godliness and dignity. This is good and pleases God our Savior, who wants everyone to be saved and to understand the truth. For, there is one God and one Mediator who can reconcile God and humanity—the man Christ Jesus. He gave his life to purchase freedom for everyone. This is the message God gave to the world at just the right time." 1 Timothy 2:1-6 (NLT)

Pray for leaders in government today. Send them an encouraging note.

Journal

Looking back on your day, describe how you met the challenge of generosity.

Journal

BE
COURAGEOUS

07 DAY

"Fear is the fence that keeps us stuck in our comfort zones."
—Alex Harris and Brett Harris

DEVOTIONAL

Bible Passage

"So be strong and courageous! Do not be afraid and do not panic before them. For the Lord your God will personally go ahead of you. He will neither fail you nor abandon you."
Deuteronomy 31:6 (NLT)

Questions

1. Reread the passage. Underline words and phrases that challenge us to live generously.

2. What fears do you have about letting go and living out a generous life? How can the promises in this verse help you?

Pray For

Others - Opportunities to get to know your neighbors.

Kindness - May my actions be filled with kindness today.

My Attitude - Create in me an attractiveness that causes people to desire relationship with me. For daily strength and courage on this journey.

Today's Selfless Act

Go for a walk around your neighborhood. Pray for your neighbors—by name if you know them. Begin asking God for opportunities to meet and get to know them.

Journal

Looking back on your day, describe how you met the challenge of generosity.

Journal

08
DAY

POWER
FOR GOOD

"You have not lived until you have done something for someone who can never repay you."—*John Bunyan*

DEVOTIONAL

Bible Passage

"Do not withhold good from those who deserve it when it's in your power to help them."
Proverbs 3:27 (NLT)

Questions

1. Reread the passage. Underline words and phrases that challenge us to live generously.

2. Can you think of a time when you withheld good from someone? Why?

3. What are some examples of helping someone that are within your power to do?

Pray For

Others - Pray for your neighbors by name.

Self Control - that I don't miss out on God's plan for my day.

My Attitude - That I would place other's needs ahead of my own today.

Today's Selfless Act

Do something good today, like helping with chores around the house.

Journal

Looking back on your day, describe how you met the challenge of generosity.

Journal

Journal

A Generous Twist Story
Pay The Bill

When you only have a few things to purchase at the grocery store it's a lot easier to go to the small neighborhood store than one of the bigger box stores. And so it happened one day I found myself bopping into the neighborhood store. I put my few items in the cart and headed toward the checkout lane. There was a woman in front of me checking out—I was next in line! There are so many things that catch your eye in that check out lane—delicious candy, mints, gums, and magazines, some with pictures of beautiful people and others with pictures of fantastic food. It's usually at this point in my shopping experience that I allow my mind to wander thinking about meals I will never make and diets that promise a slim figure if you are willing to just eat bananas.

This time, however, as my mind was in that state of nothingness, I overheard the cashier say, "That will be $75.92." The woman in front of me only had $50.00. She seemed surprised that the groceries could cost that much—the look on her face almost accusing the cashier of overcharging her.

It was then that I heard, or rather sensed, God say to me, "Buy her groceries."

What? I don't know her, I've never seen her before in our neighborhood store. She isn't asking for help. She's appears to be angry. What will she think when I offer to pay for her groceries? What will the people around me think? I came to the store to purchase a few things for myself, not to purchase someone else's groceries.

And then, there it was again, that soft nudging in my spirit, "Cover the rest of the cost of her groceries."

Here's the deal. Personally, we didn't have that much cash. As missionaries, during this period of our lives our faith was being tested and God was stretching us. We were learning what it meant to totally depend on God to supply our every need. Not our wants, but our needs. We prayed daily that God would supply our needs. We researched George Mueller's life, the great missionary in England who prayed about everything and expected each prayer to be answered. He prayed for God to supply for the needs of his 5 orphanages. And God did. Many times, Mueller received unsolicited food donations only hours before they were needed to feed the children. And God was supplying what we needed. But it wasn't like we had a huge savings account that we could dip into when the end of the month came and we needed just a little bit more. There was no emergency fund stashed under some mattress. This woman didn't look like she needed my help with her groceries. It wasn't like she had 3 small children with her who looked so lovable that you would want to give them the world. There wasn't time for me to look at her groceries to see if what she was buying was essential—like milk and toilet paper. Maybe she was buying unnecessary things! Didn't this stranger in front of me have options? Couldn't she put some of her groceries back on the shelf or get more money out of the ATM machine?

I could not shake the feeling that I was supposed to help pay for her groceries. Really, Lord? She's a stranger. She's different than me. Does she really need my help? I wasn't even sure that I would have enough cash for my groceries if I paid for hers.

I remember keeping my head down as I softly said, "I'll pay the rest." And I took the money out of my wallet and gave it to the cashier.

I wish you could have been there when I handed over the money. I wish you could have seen the reaction of the woman and the cashier. But I'm glad you weren't there because there was no reaction. The woman didn't turn to me with a big smile on her face and say, "Thank you so much for helping me buy this food." She didn't say anything. She didn't acknowledge me at all. She just took her groceries and left the store. The cashier then proceeded to check out my groceries and I left the store a bit puzzled.

Wasn't there supposed to be an acknowledgment of the gift given? Weren't you supposed to feel joy in helping others?

The point of this story isn't about how wonderful a person I am for helping someone in need because, unfortunately, I am too often consumed with my own needs to notice the needs of others. The point is I must be obedient to what the Lord requires of me. I must give because that's what the Lord asks of me. I must be willing to give generously even if I don't think I have enough. I must be willing to give without knowing the end result. I must be willing to live generously without receiving any accolades.

If I truly wish to be a part of a generous community I need to understand that it starts with me. I can't wait for others to begin the process. I can't let others' reactions dictate how I move forward. Live generously. Give generously. And, if you want to see a great example of how to do that, take some time to read about Jesus.

09 DAY

DO GOOD

"We make a living by what we get; we make a life by what we give."
—Winston Churchill

DEVOTIONAL

Bible Passage

"And don't forget to do good and to share with those in need. These are the sacrifices that please God."
Hebrews 13:16 (NLT)

Questions

1. Reread the passage. Underline words and phrases that challenge us to live generously.

2. Make a list of things people have shared with you.

Pray For

Others - Pray for my circle of influence* - their homes, families, their hearts to be open to Jesus.

Gentleness - In my actions with others.

My Attitude - That I will be able to genuinely listen to people today and care for their needs.

Today's Selfless Act

Share some precious time with a neighbor or someone from work.

*Note: Your circle of influence is the circle of people around you that you connect with on a regular basis. They include your family members, co-workers, cohorts, neighbors, fellow students, church buddies, etc.

Journal

Looking back on your day, describe how you met the challenge of generosity.

Journal

ANOTHER
CHANCE

"At the start of the day
I lift my hands to say
Thank You Lord for another chance to worship You.
Every minute, every hour
I'm gonna say it louder
Thank You Lord for another chance to worship You
You've been good."
—*"Another Chance" by Ken Reynolds*

DEVOTIONAL

Bible Passage

"This is the day the Lord has made.
We will rejoice and be glad in it."
Psalm 118:24 (NLT)

Questions

1. Reread the passage. Underline words and phrases that challenge us to live generously.

2. What does worshipping the Lord look like to you?

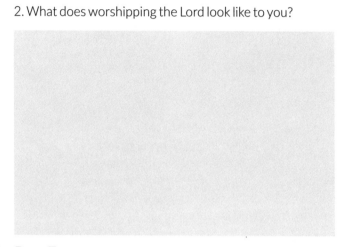

 **Pray For**

Others - For my neighbors- their needs and families.

Self Control - That I would put aside my wants and seek only You, Lord.

My Attitude - That I would use every hour today to truly worship You, Lord.

Today's Selfless Act

Today is another chance to worship God. Set the alarm on your cell phone to ring every hour and then take a moment to worship God where you are.

Journal

Looking back on your day, describe how you met the challenge of generosity.

Journal

11
DAY

ONE LORD

*"We are settling for a Christianity that revolves around catering to
ourselves when the central message of Christianity is actually about
abandoning ourselves." — David Platt*

 Bible Passage

"But for us,
There is one God, the Father,
by whom all things were created,
and for whom we live.

And there is one Lord, Jesus Christ,
through whom all things were created,
and through whom we live."
1 Corinthians 8:6 (NLT)

(?) Questions

1. Reread the passage. Underline words and phrases that challenge
us to live generously.

2. God created everything. What are some of your favorite places in God's creation?

Pray For

Others - Pastors and missionaries who are serving the Lord.

Joy - In all God created - celebrate His creative design.

My Attitude - Allow me to abandon the stress of the day and focus wholly on You, Lord.

Today's Selfless Act

Grab a friend and spend time today in God's creation.

Journal

Looking back on your day, describe how you met the challenge of generosity.

Journal

BROKEN

Relationships are tricky. If we are going to be intentionally generous in our relationship with others, we have to be willing to open ourselves up to hurt, conflict, and brokenness. If you've been hurt in the past, rest assured that God will bring healing. Don't let that hurt keep you from developing new relationships and restoring old relationships. When we intentionally reach out to others we also open ourselves up to the possibility of amazing relationships of hope, friendship, and encouragement.

DEVOTIONAL

Bible Passage

"He heals the brokenhearted
and binds up their wounds.
He determines the number of the stars
and calls them each by name.
Great is our Lord and mighty in power;
his understanding has no limit."
Psalm 147:3-5 (NIV)

? Questions

1. Reread the passage. Underline words and phrases that challenge us to live generously.

2. Take time today to honestly look at the relationships you have with others. Thank God for those relationships that breathe life into you. Ask God to bring healing to those that are broken.

Pray For

Others - Friends who are hurting, may they find healing in You, Lord.

Peace - In the midst of broken relationships.

My Attitude - Heal my heart where it has been broken so I can be a blessing to others.

Today's Selfless Act

Reach out to someone who is hurting today. Send them a text or email, call them, or go out for coffee or ice cream together.

Journal

Looking back on your day, describe how you met the challenge of generosity.

Journal

BLESSED
TO GIVE

"Give naught, get same. Give much, get same."
—Malcolm Forbes, American publisher

Bible Passage

"And I have been a constant example of how you can help those in need by working hard. You should remember the words of the Lord Jesus: 'It is more blessed to give than to receive.'"
Acts 20:35 (NLT)

Questions

1. Reread the passage. Underline words and phrases that challenge us to live generously.

2. Why is it more blessed to give than to receive?

Pray For

Others - My friends, that their needs would be met today.

Goodness - Allow my actions to overflow with goodness toward others.

My Attitude - Lord, give me a generous spirit where both my eyes and hands are open for You today.

Today's Selfless Act

Look for opportunities to give today: your time, money, and talents. Be generous with it all!

Journal

Looking back on your day, describe how you met the challenge of generosity.

Journal

Journal

A Generous Twist Story
A Generous Heart

What does a generous heart look like? Here's one story:

The truck pulled up in front of our house.

"Is this 2211 Pamela Place?"
"Yes."
"I have a new washing machine in my truck for you."
"What? We didn't buy a washing machine!"
"Well, somebody did and I'm supposed to deliver it, set it up, and take away the old machine."

Two days earlier we were standing in our laundry room wondering what to do. Our washing machine had just quit working. There was no money to buy a new machine. Janet suggested borrowing money from her Dad so we could purchase a good used machine. But we honestly didn't know how we would repay him. Bob suggested we ask our Heavenly Father instead. So we took a moment right there in our laundry room and asked the Lord to provide a washing machine for us.

And today a brand new washing machine showed up at our door. Praise God! A generous soul purchased a brand new washing machine for us AND paid to have the old, broken machine taken away! That's the act of selflessness. Generously giving. Anonymously. No credit, no honor, just a generous heart.

Oh that we might we have a generous heart that generously gives.

WHATEVER

DAY 14

"Great opportunities often disguise themselves in small tasks."
—Rick Warren

········· DEVOTIONAL

Bible Passage

"And let the peace that comes from Christ rule in your hearts. For as members of one body you are called to live in peace. And always be thankful. Let the message about Christ, in all its richness, fill your lives. Teach and counsel each other with all the wisdom he gives. Sing psalms and hymns and spiritual songs to God with thankful hearts. And whatever you do or say, do it as a representative of the Lord Jesus, giving thanks through him to God the Father."
Colossians 3:15-17 (NLT)

Questions

1. Reread the passage. Underline words and phrases that challenge us to live generously.

2. Self check: in your "saying and doing" how well are you representing the Lord Jesus? What areas need improvement?

Pray For

Others - For my neighbors - that their homes, families, and hearts would be open to Jesus.

Faithfulness - In my words and deeds, that they would match up.

My Attitude - Jesus help me represent You well today in all that I say, do and think.

Today's Selfless Act

Focus today on the words that you use; be thankful, encourage others, speak peace, share wisdom.

Journal

Looking back on your day, describe how you met the challenge of generosity.

Journal

15 DAY

CONTENTMENT:
BUY ONE
GIVE ONE

"Those who have much need more." —Sudanese Pastor

"We must learn to be content with what we've been given versus always wanting the upgrade. Technology has taught us to lust after the upgrade." —Bob Wielenga

········ **DEVOTIONAL**

Bible Passage

"Everything is wearisome beyond description. No matter how much we see, we are never satisfied. No matter how much we hear, we are not content."
Ecclesiastes 1:8 (NLT)

Questions

1. Reread the passage. Underline words and phrases that challenge us to live generously.

2. How satisfied are you? Explain.

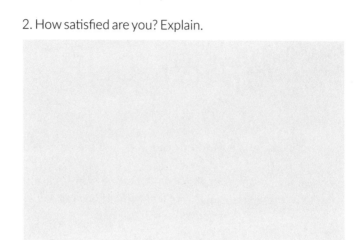

Pray For

Others - Family members to find strength and joy today.

Patience - With what I've been entrusted with so I don't chase headlong after things that don't matter.

My Attitude - May my heart be content in everything today.

Today's Selfless Act

No social media today; instead, gather some people together and play a game.

Journal

Looking back on your day, describe how you met the challenge of generosity.

Journal

LOVE GOD

"God proved His love on the Cross. When Christ hung, and bled, and died, it was God saying to the world, 'I love you.'" —Billy Graham

DEVOTIONAL

Bible Passage

"Teacher, which is the greatest commandment in the Law?" Jesus replied: 'Love the Lord your God with all your heart and with all your soul and with all your mind.' This is the first and greatest commandment. And the second is like it: 'Love your neighbor as yourself.'"
Matthew 22:36-39 (NIV)

Questions

1. Reread the passage. Underline words and phrases that challenge us to live generously.

2. How do you show God that you love Him?

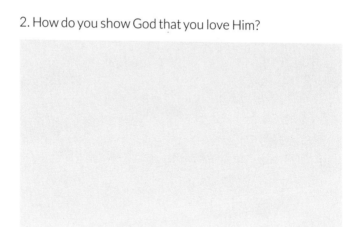

Pray For

Others - Neighbors and coworkers to see the love of Christ in me today.

Love - Not just for those I like but for those I struggle with as well.

My Attitude - Lord help me love You more so that others begin to see the overflow of that love.

Today's Selfless Act

Spend 15 minutes alone with God today—pray, sing, and read the Bible. Let Him know how much you love Him. Write out today's Bible passage and commit it to memory.

Journal

Looking back on your day, describe how you met the challenge of generosity.

Journal

17 DAY

LOVE PEOPLE

"Do you know that nothing you do in this life will ever matter, unless it is about loving God and loving the people he has made?" - Francis Chan

Bible Passage

"Jesus said: ' This is my commandment: Love each other in the same way I have loved you. There is no greater love than to lay down one's life for one's friends.'"
John 15:12-13 (NLT)

Questions

1. Reread the passage. Underline words and phrases that challenge us to live generously.

2. How do you show love to others?

Pray For

Others - Marriage relationships to be filled with love, forgiveness, and kindness.

Kindness - Toward all today, especially toward those who frustrate me.

My Attitude - Help me to see past the outward expression of people and help me see them the way You do, Lord.

Today's Selfless Act

Show love today by spending time with someone and really listening to them—take a walk, play with their children, buy them coffee, sit and chat together.

Journal

Looking back on your day, describe how you met the challenge of generosity.

Journal

EXCEL, EXCEED,
OUTDO

"It's not how much we give but how much love we put into giving."
— Mother Teresa

 Bible Passage

"But since you excel in everything—in faith, in speech, in knowledge, in complete earnestness and in the love we have kindled in you—see that you also excel in this grace of giving." 2 Corinthians 8:7 (NIV)

Questions

1. Reread the passage. Underline words and phrases that challenge us to live generously.

2. What would it look like for you to excel in the gracious act of giving?

Pray For

Others - Those who are homeless, may they find shelter and food.

Gentleness - Help me learn how to express the gentle grace of giving.

My Attitude - Help me not get caught up in the doing but in the reason behind the doing.

Today's Selfless Act

Buy a meal for a stranger today.

Journal

Looking back on your day, describe how you met the challenge of generosity.

Journal

A Generous Twist Story
Pasta Dinner

Our son Jon and his wife Lynn-Holly began hosting Thursday Night Pasta Dinners because they wanted to find a way to bring multiple friend groups together. Here's their story:

Being a voracious reader of blogs, Lynn-Holly came across a writer describing a pasta dinner she regularly hosted. Feeling inspired, we thought it would be a great opportunity to connect people within the community to one another.

We always wanted our home to be a welcoming place and so when we finally had the space in our home (a 1200 square foot, 3 bedroom house) to host groups for dinner, we hoped to do it in a fun and unique way.

We invited people from all of our circles of influence—our local coffee shop, the yoga studio, church small groups, and graduate students; no one was purposefully excluded. We asked that people give us a 24 hour RSVP notice if they were coming to ensure we had made enough pasta and meatballs.

Sometimes we would intentionally invite married couples one week when we knew we had a new couple to Waco coming as well. We had multiple couple friends with infants and toddlers that we thought would become great friends (And they did!). Not everyone was believers, but we thought we could introduce thoughtful conversation topics and see where the dialogue went from there. This derived from reading Sheldon Vanuaken's book, *A Severe Mercy*, about how C.S. Lewis and he would have wine nights with friends and would spend hours discussing deeper issues, ranging from theological to social and political.

Lynn-Holly would make homemade meatballs from her own recipe (that were delicious!) and together we would make the pasta.

For anyone that would come to pasta dinner, we asked that they would bring a side dish to pass. It could be anything, ranging from a bag of chips to crudités, or salad, sweet tea, or even desserts. People brought strawberries, muffins, wine, egg rolls, and fresh produce from their own garden!

We only had one table, but we had TV trays and it seemed like the conversations would typically happen in 3 groups. One group ate at the table, and two different conversations would happen in the living room between the couches, chairs, and ottomans. We didn't facilitate much of the socializing besides making sure each person was introduced to everyone else in the house, and we would try to share anything we thought two strangers had in common.

Pasta Dinner

At the end of the 40 days you will be asked to host a simple gathering for a group of 6-12 people. First, get rid of any fears of your home not being big enough or nice enough. Getting together with others is not about your house—it's about being with people. And, just in case you're not a big people person, this is your chance to grab a friend who loves people and host a gathering together.

Make a list of who to invite to Pasta night. Prayerfully ask God who you should invite. Think about how many people you could host—don't worry about seats for everyone. Invite a mixture of people—some you know well and others you don't know as well. Be intentional about who you invite. Think of things this group of people might have in common.

Your gathering doesn't have to be elaborate. Paper plates work just as well fine china. You can do dinner or dessert. We've discovered that pasta is a simple meal and it's something most people like. You can even cook gluten free pasta for those with dietary needs. It's easy to order pizza or cook hot dogs. Ice Cream Sundaes are also easy and fun! If you want to make cookies or bread, be sure to involve your family members or housemates. You have the option of providing everything or ask those you invite to bring something to share.

19
DAY

TAKE
ACTION

"Too often we assume God has increased our income to increase our standard of living when His stated purpose is to increase our standard of giving." — Randy Alcorn

 ## Bible Passage

"What good is it, my brothers and sisters, if someone claims to have faith but has no deeds? Can such faith save them? Suppose a brother or a sister is without clothes and daily food. 'If one of you says to them', 'Go in peace; keep warm and well fed', but does nothing about their physical needs, what good is it? In the same way, faith by itself, if it is not accompanied by action, is dead."
James 2:14-17 (NIV)

 ## Questions

1. Reread the passage. Underline words and phrases that challenge us to live generously.

2. Have you ever received food or clothing from someone? How did it make you feel?

Pray For

Others - For those in my circle of influence*— their homes, families, hearts to be open to Jesus.

Kindness - Give me the chance to be extravagantly kind with someone today.

My Attitude - Help me look past myself and truly become selfless in my attitude and actions

Today's Selfless Act

Collect and donate food to a local food bank today. While there, put a date on your calendar to help serve.

*Note: Your circle of influence is the circle of people around you that you connect with on a regular basis. They include your family members, co-workers, cohorts, neighbors, fellow students, church buddies, etc.

Journal

Looking back on your day, describe how you met the challenge of generosity.

Journal

20 DAY

KEEP ON

"Our prayers may be awkward. Our attempts may be feeble. But since the power of prayer is in the one who hears it and not in the one who says it, our prayers do make a difference." —Max Lucado

.... DEVOTIONAL

Bible Passage

"Keep on asking, and you will receive what you ask for. Keep on seeking, and you will find. Keep on knocking, and the door will be opened to you. For everyone who asks, receives. Everyone who seeks, finds. And to everyone who knocks, the door will be opened."
Matthew 7:7-8 (NLT)

Questions

1. Reread the passage. Underline words and phrases that challenge us to live generously.

2. When have times of prayer made a difference in your life?

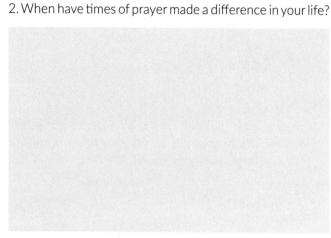

 **Pray For**

Others - That the world may know Jesus-His love, forgiveness, and salvation through Him.

Love - Help me to really love others by seeing people as they are and praying for their needs.

My Attitude - Lord, teach me to cry out to you on behalf of others the way I would pray for myself.

Today's Selfless Act

As you're out and about today listen to what is going on around you, pray for all the people you see- be specific.

Journal

Looking back on your day, describe how you met the challenge of generosity.

Journal

ENCOURAGE
ONE ANOTHER

"The measure of a life is not its duration, but its donation."
— Peter Marshall, former U.S. Senate chaplain

DEVOTIONAL

Bible Passage

"So encourage each other and build each other up, just as you are already doing."
1 Thessalonians 5:11 (NLT)

Questions

1. Reread the passage. Underline words and phrases that challenge us to live generously.

2. What do you find encouraging?

3. How do you encourage others?

Pray For

Others - Family members, may they be encouraged today.

Joy - May I find joy and bring joy to others as I encourage them today.

My Attitude - Remind me Lord throughout the day to be encouraging in those moments when I might be caustic instead.

 ## Today's Selfless Act

Encourage someone in your family today. Make them some cookies or send them a personal note.

 ## Journal

Looking back on your day, describe how you met the challenge of generosity.

Journal

22 DAY

GOD'S PEACE

"You will find it necessary to let things go, simply for the reason that they are too heavy." - Corrie ten Boom

Bible Passage

"Don't worry about anything; instead, pray about everything. Tell God what you need, and thank him for all he has done. Then you will experience God's peace, which exceeds anything we can understand. His peace will guard your hearts and minds as you live in Christ Jesus."
Philippians 4:6-7 (NLT)

Questions

1. Reread the passage. Underline words and phrases that challenge us to live generously.

2. What are you worried about today?

3. How can God bring peace in your worry?

 Pray For

Others - Those in my circle of influence to experience God's peace today.

Patience - May I patiently abide in Christ today.

My Attitude - May I have opportunities throughout today to lift someone's spirit and provide comfort in the midst of their anxiety.

Today's Selfless Act

Do you know someone who is worried? Let them know you care. Contact them and pray for them (out loud-together!). Arrange a coffee date with them to get together within the next 5 days.

Journal

Looking back on your day, describe how you met the challenge of generosity.

Journal

23 DAY

PRACTICE
HOSPITALITY

*"...often, stepping outside your comfort zone is not careless
irresponsibility, but a necessary act of obedience."*
—Andy Stanley

 ### Bible Passage

"Don't just pretend to love others. Really love them. Hate what
is wrong. Hold tightly to what is good...When God's people are
in need, be ready to help them. Always be eager to practice
hospitality."
Romans 12:9,13 (NLT)

 ### Questions

1. Reread the passage. Underline words and phrases that challenge
us to live generously.

2. What are you holding tightly to?

3. What does it mean to practice hospitality?

 Pray For

Others - Those in my circle of influence to experience God's love today.

Goodness - Give me grace to know how good it is when we encourage one another through our hospitality.

My Attitude - Help me care more about people than how my house looks.

Today's Selfless Act

Practice hospitality today. Invite people over to your home for dinner or dessert (pasta night, pizza night, pancake night—it doesn't have to be a gourmet dinner!).

 ## Journal

Looking back on your day, describe how you met the challenge of generosity.

Journal

SEND ME

"I used to think you had to be special for God to use you, but now I know you simply need to say yes." —Bob Goff

········ DEVOTIONAL

Bible Passage

"Then I heard the voice of the Lord saying, 'Whom shall I send? And who will go for us?' And I said, 'Here am I. Send me!'"
Isaiah 6:8 (NIV)

Questions

1. Reread the passage. Underline words and phrases that challenge us to live generously.

2. As you look back over your life, when did you say "yes" to God?

Pray For

Others - Pray for your neighbors— their homes, families, hearts to be open to Jesus and the opportunities to connect with them.

Self Control - Lord, help me learn how to say "Yes".

My Attitude - Help me to be quick to help, slow to say no, and available today when needed.

Today's Selfless Act

Live generously today! Say yes to what God lays upon your heart. Set the alarm on your cell phone to ring every hour. Ask God what He wants you to say "yes" to regarding living generously. Then do it!

Journal

Looking back on your day, describe how you met the challenge of generosity.

Journal

A Generous Twist Story
In the Midst of a Hurricane

2004 was an interesting year for the Casteel family. Listen in as Eric tells their story.

At the time we were living in South Florida and expecting our second child. We had lived in the area a few years and knew that eventually we would experience a real hurricane. We did not expect it to be during the birth of our second child, nor did we know that it would not be one but three major hurricanes that would strike that summer.

Life in suburban Florida is a busy one. The cost of living is high and there is very much a sense of keeping up with the Joneses. We lived in a great community near the beach and loved the lifestyle we were able to afford. We attended a great church and were trying to forge meaningful relationships and grow spiritually. When the forecast of the storms came the community really united and helped one another out. I remember a group of men from our church working for about 20 hours straight to help put storm shutters up throughout the neighborhood to beat the coming storm surge. It felt good to help others in need and see the community come together when it mattered most.

After the first storm we were out of power for almost 3 weeks and the water was bad for some time. Most of the stores ran out of supplies and for quite a while you couldn't even get gas. Looking back, the storm's impact on our everyday lives exposed how fragile our very busy lifestyle really was. Losing access to things like readily available food and water, electricity, banking, and gas for even a short period of time brought our lives to a screeching halt.

Guess what happened though when our lives were put on pause for just a few weeks? Our neighbors, all of them, came together and shared what they had and made sure everybody had adequate food and water. Neighbors we ashamedly didn't even know the names of were checking in to see if we were alright. We came together and really lived as a true community sharing and meeting one another's needs.. In many cases it was the first time we were able to really get to know those we lived right next to.

When I look back on my life I don't view these "crisis" times as "hard" times. Hard times for me are often when I am over scheduled and too busy. Too busy to even recognize the needs of those who live around me. In reality I remember that hurricane summer as one of the best summers of my life. In fact during the second hurricane, literally while the storm was overhead, the power out and no air conditioning, my daughter Kathryn was born. We had all sorts of help from the community despite the fact none of our family were able to be there due to the storm.

During a crisis like this an entire community is forced stop their over-scheduled busy lives and, in that void of time that is created, we recognize the needs of others. When we recognize the needs of others we are able to be who we were created to be - we are able to truly love our neighbor.

REAPING A
HARVEST

*"Sometimes the greatest act of faith is faithfulness, staying
where you're planted." — Craig Groeschel*

········ **DEVOTIONAL**

"

Bible Passage

"Let us not become weary in doing good, for at the proper time
we will reap a harvest if we do not give up. Therefore, as we have
opportunity, let us do good to all people, especially to those
who belong to the family of believers."
Galatians 6:9-10 (NIV)

Questions

1. Reread the passage. Underline words and phrases that challenge
us to live generously.

2. How is your harvest coming along?

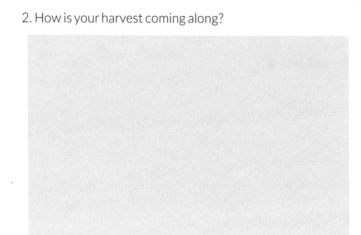

Pray For

Others - Believers around the world.

Peace - In the midst of everyone else's chaos today, may I bring Your peace.

My Attitude - God, I'm busy. Life is hectic, but help me to never tire of doing good for Your sake.

Today's Selfless Act

Think of someone you know who is weary. Think of a way to encourage them in the ministry God is calling them to do—it could be as simple as an encouraging text or phone call, offering to clean their house, or buying them a gift card and personally delivering it.

Journal

Looking back on your day, describe how you met the challenge of generosity.

Journal

TAKE UP
YOUR CROSS

"Any person who only sticks with Christianity as long as things are going his or her way, is a stranger to the cross." — Tim Keller

DEVOTIONAL

 Bible Passage

"Then, calling the crowd to join his disciples, he said, 'If any of you wants to be my follower, you must give up your own way, take up your cross, and follow me'. If you try to hang on to your life, you will lose it. But if you give up your life for my sake and for the sake of the Good News, you will save it. And what do you benefit if you gain the whole world but lose your own soul?'"
Mark 8:34-36 (NLT)

(?) **Questions**

1. Reread the passage. Underline words and phrases that challenge us to live generously.

2. What does it mean to give up your life for Jesus' sake and for the sake of the Good News?

Pray For

Others - Persecuted Christians around the world.

Faithfulness - Help me to be faithful in spending time with You today.

My Attitude - Help me to focus on You in the midst of life, work, school, the mess, and the chaos.

Today's Selfless Act

Spend 15 minutes alone with God today—no interruptions. Meditate on today's Bible passage. Ask God to reveal to you the things you are trying to hang on to or gain that are pulling you away from Him. Renew your commitment to following Him.

Journal

Looking back on your day, describe how you met the challenge of generosity.

Journal

CHURCH

"Church is not a spectator sport. In fact, you cannot go to church because you are the church. Church is not a building with a specific address. Church is not a gathering at a certain time. If you are the church, then church is happening whenever and wherever you are! You take the presence of God with you wherever you go." —Mark Batterson

Bible Passage

"But you are the ones chosen by God, chosen for the high calling of priestly work, chosen to be a holy people, God's instruments to do his work and speak out for him, to tell others of the night-and-day difference he made for you—from nothing to something, from rejected to accepted."
1 Peter 2:9-10 (MSG)

Questions

1. Reread the passage. Underline words and phrases that challenge us to live generously.

2. You are chosen by God! Take a moment to tell God how thankful you are!

Pray For

Others - The members of your church.

Gentleness - Help me be a gentle reminder to others of Your presence.

My Attitude - Remind me today how special I am in Your eyes, that you chose me as special and set apart for You.

Today's Selfless Act

Share your story today with 3 different people of how God has changed you "from nothing to something, from rejected to accepted."
1 Peter 2:9 (MSG)

Journal

Looking back on your day, describe how you met the challenge of generosity.

Journal

ALWAYS

"The Dead Sea is the dead sea because it continually receives and never gives." —Anonymous

Bible Passage

"Always be joyful. Never stop praying. Be thankful in all circumstances, for this is God's will for you who belong to Christ Jesus."
1 Thessalonians 5:16-18 (NLT)

Questions

1. Reread the passage. Underline words and phrases that challenge us to live generously.

2. What brings you joy?

 **Pray For**

Others - My circle of influence to experience God's joy today.

Joy - Help me to express joy when I'm with others, even in difficult situations.

My Attitude - Help me to be thankful in all circumstances today.

Today's Selfless Act

Spread some joy today—be kind to others, pray out loud with a friend, let people know you are thankful for them.

Journal

Looking back on your day, describe how you met the challenge of generosity.

Journal

INFINITELY
MORE

"Will you surrender your plans and purposes into the greater known of God's unknown designs for your life?"
—Priscilla Shirer

Bible Passage

"When I think of all this, I fall to my knees and pray to the Father, the Creator of everything in heaven and on earth. I pray that from his glorious, unlimited resources he will empower you with inner strength through his Spirit. Then Christ will make his home in your hearts as you trust in him. Your roots will grow down into God's love and keep you strong. And may you have the power to understand, as all God's people should, how wide, how long, how high, and how deep his love is. May you experience the love of Christ, though it is too great to understand fully. Then you will be made complete with all the fullness of life and power that comes from God.

Now all glory to God, who is able, through his mighty power at work within us, to accomplish infinitely more than we might ask or think."
Ephesians 3:14-20 (NLT)

Questions

1. Reread the passage. Underline words and phrases that challenge us to live generously.

2. Write down examples from your life when God accomplished infinitely more than you could ask or imagine.

 ## Pray For

Others - That the World may experience how wide, long, high, and deep the love of God is.

Self Control - Help me to seek Your face and allow Christ to make his home in my heart.

My Attitude - Let today be about You, Lord and not about me.

 ## Today's Selfless Act

Reread today's Bible passage as a prayer for 5 different people in your life: A neighbor, a coworker, a family member, a missionary, and a friend:

I pray that from his glorious, unlimited resources he will empower _____ with inner strength through his Spirit. Then Christ will make his home in_____ hearts as you trust in him.

Your roots will grow down into God's love and keep _____ strong. And may_____ have the power to understand, as all God's people should, how wide, how long, how high, and how deep his love is. May _____ experience the love of Christ, though it is too great to understand fully. Then_____ will be made complete with all the fullness of life and power that comes from God.

Now all glory to God, who is able, through his mighty power at work within us, to accomplish infinitely more than we might ask or think.

Journal

Looking back on your day, describe how you met the challenge of generosity.

Journal

A Generous Twist Story
Becoming Like a Child

When Eric and Amy's oldest daughter was very young she was diagnosed with a medical condition that required multiple surgeries to correct. This meant spending more time than any of them really wanted in hospitals getting the medical attention she needed. One particular situation during that time greatly impacted their lives. Here's their story.

Our daughter always had a problem with getting an IV to work right. Her little veins just didn't want to receive the needle. One night she needed to have an IV put in and the medical team took her with my wife to the "procedure room", a place where they took kids to deal with needles and other things they needed that might be scary for the children. At night in our hospital room you could hear kids in the procedure room crying and struggling and then taken back to their room. On this particular night our daughter was in that room for over three hours. My wife had to hold her down to get the IV in. It was a very difficult time as parents.

That was my night to sleep at the hospital with our little girl. At about 2 a.m. I looked over at her with the moonlight on her sad tired face. I asked her if she was ok. She told me she was listening to the child scream and cry in the procedure room. To be honest I hadn't really noticed. Then I listened and heard. When asked why she was so sad my little girl of about four said something that blew me away. She said, "We need to pray for the little girl struggling in the procedure room. She doesn't realize that the doctors are trying to help her.

I couldn't believe what she said. She didn't complain about her situation or the pain and struggle she was enduring. She wasn't focused on herself at all, rather her focus was on a stranger struggling with something she could identify with. You see she had accepted her struggle and simply trusted that God was in control.

Her response to this was an empathetic understanding of what another person was going through. And her heart knew the best thing to do was to pray that the child in the procedure room would realize she was not alone and that God was there with her. She would have peace that all would be OK.

As a church it is critical to understand that if we are to be a catalyst for developing healthy community and a relevant light in the world we must understand who we are before the Father. When we focus on being children of God, wholly dependent on him, we are able to better love and embrace the journey our neighbors are on. Rather than a preoccupation on our own struggle to achieve status and meaning through our own efforts, we are able to empathize and identify with the struggles of life. Maybe we are supposed to be like my daughter. Instead of being consumed by the difficulties of our life - we are instead, consumed by the struggle of others. Understanding that unless they too see themselves as a loved child of God they may never be able to come to terms with whatever struggle life has dealt them.

This is the power of the message of the gospel. A full acceptance of the pardon offered by Christ on the cross and a recognition that as a believer we hold the most revered position in all of creation - that of being a loved child of God. Without a church that is reflecting this and living it out in our local community the world will never see what a life of sustained joy and love really looks like. Without a vibrant church there cannot be a truly vibrant community.

I hope my daughter never loses the innocence she had that night in the hospital. The challenge for myself and others is to ask: are we more consumed with our own difficulties rather than being concerned with the obstacles others are facing today? And if so - what impact is that having on the people we interact with on a daily basis? Maybe we all need to wake up each day and recognize that we are valued and loved children of God. It is only from here that we as believers can reflect the Kingdom of God, to the community in which we belong.

BE LIKE JESUS

"Don't be afraid. Just have faith." —Jesus, Mark 5:36 (NLT)

 Bible Passage

"Is there any encouragement from belonging to Christ? Any comfort from his love? Any fellowship together in the Spirit? Are your hearts tender and compassionate? Then make me truly happy by agreeing wholeheartedly with each other, loving one another, and working together with one mind and purpose. Don't be selfish; don't try to impress others. Be humble, thinking of others as better than yourselves. Don't look out only for your own interests, but take an interest in others, too. You must have the same attitude that Christ Jesus had."
Philippians 2:1-5 (NLT)

(?) **Questions**

1. Reread the passage. Underline words and phrases that challenge us to live generously.

2. Would people describe you as compassionate, humble, and interested in others' lives? Why or why not?

Pray For

Others - Friends to love one another and work together.

Kindness - Help me to show kindness to all I meet today, looking out for other's interests instead of my own.

My Attitude - Lord, help me to walk in unity and humility. Show me how to have the same attitude that Jesus had.

Today's Selfless Act

In every opportunity today, put other's needs before your own—open doors for people, listen first before speaking, ask someone what they did last night, let someone go in front of you at a restaurant or grocery store, instead of buying something for yourself, purchase it and give it away.

Journal

Looking back on your day, describe how you met the challenge of generosity.

Journal

DAY 31   GOLDEN RULE

"Whatever one of us asked the other to do - it was assumed the asker would weigh all the consequences - the other would do. Thus one might wake the other in the night and ask for a cup of water; and the other would peacefully (and sleepily) fetch it. We, in fact, defined courtesy as 'a cup of water in the night'. And we considered it a very great courtesy to ask for the cup as well as to fetch it."
—Sheldon Vanauken

DEVOTIONAL

Bible Passage

"Do to others as you would like them to do to you."
Luke 6:31 (NLT)

Questions

1. Reread the passage. Underline words and phrases that challenge us to live generously.

2. Sheldon Vanauken and his wife defined courtesy as a 'cup of water in the night'. How would you define courtesy?

Pray For

Others - My circle of influence to experience God today.

Patience - Give me patience for each encounter I face today.

My Attitude - Help me to see others' needs as more important than my own.

Today's Selfless Act

Go through a drive thru sometime today and pay for the car behind you. If there isn't a car behind you, purchase a gift card to give to a stranger.

Journal

Looking back on your day, describe how you met the challenge of generosity.

Journal

LOVE IS AN
ACTION WORD

"How wonderful it is that nobody need wait a single moment before starting to improve the world." —Anne Frank

 Bible Passage

"Dear children, let's not merely say that we love each other; let us show the truth by our actions. Our actions will show that we belong to the truth, so we will be confident when we stand before God."
1 John 3:18-19 (NLT)

? Questions

1. Reread the passage. Underline words and phrases that challenge us to live generously.

2. What are some ways to show truth and love by our actions?

Pray For

Others - Believers around the world to truly love others.

Love - Lord, fill my heart with love for others.

My Attitude - Help me to live out my faith by my actions, taking advantage of opportunities You place before me to show love.

Today's Selfless Act

Show love today by baking cookies, bread, a meal, or something else for a neighbor or coworker.

Journal

Looking back on your day, describe how you met the challenge of generosity.

Journal

OVERFLOWING
GENEROSITY

"Never doubt that a small group of thoughtful, committed, citizens can change the world." —Margaret Mead

········ **DEVOTIONAL**

 ## Bible Passage

"Now I want you to know, dear brothers and sisters, what God in his kindness has done through the churches in Macedonia. They are being tested by many troubles, and they are very poor. But they are also filled with abundant joy, which has overflowed in rich generosity.

For I can testify that they gave not only what they could afford, but far more. And they did it of their own free will. They begged us again and again for the privilege of sharing in the gift for the believers in Jerusalem. They even did more than we had hoped, for their first action was to give themselves to the Lord and to us, just as God wanted them to do."
2 Corinthians 8:1-5 (NLT)

 ## Questions

1. Reread the passage. Underline words and phrases that challenge us to live generously.

2. Why do you think the Macedonians begged for the privilege of sharing in the gift for the believers in Jerusalem?

 Pray For

Others - Pray for your neighbors— their homes, families, and hearts to be open to Jesus.

Peace - Help me to experience peace as I freely share what has been given to me.

My Attitude - Give me a joyful heart that is overflowing in generosity.

 Today's Selfless Act

Give a generous gift to a church or other ministry God has placed on your heart.

Journal

Looking back on your day, describe how you met the challenge of generosity.

Journal

Journal

A Generous Twist Story
I'd Like a Large Coffee To Go

Traveling in a car with Rick meant you would always be stopping at Dunkin' Donuts because, in his words, "No one should ever have to ride in a car without something to eat and drink." I remember as we rolled through the drive thru I made the mistake of ordering a medium coffee. Rick looked at me and said, "If a large costs only 10 cents more why would you ever ask for a medium?" Since he was buying I changed my order to a large coffee. I didn't know it then but I've since realized that Rick was teaching me about living generously.

Rick and I traveled a lot together doing mission trips. One time we traveled to Guatemala. While there we were invited to lunch at the home of the National Director of Youth For Christ. Entering the kitchen, Rick opened the refrigerator only to find boxes of cereal stacked inside. Upon asking why you would store cereal in a refrigerator we found out that the unit hadn't worked for quite some time and was now simply being used as a cabinet. We left their home and Rick asked me where we could purchase a refrigerator. Buying a refrigerator wasn't the purpose of our trip to Guatemala and it wasn't in the budget. It meant traveling back to Guatemala City with all its traffic and noise and finding an appliance store. It meant negotiating a good price using hand gestures since neither one of us spoke Spanish.

So of course, later that day a new refrigerator was ordered and would be delivered to their home. If you asked Rick why he bought the refrigerator his answer would have sounded a lot like, "They needed one." Implied in Rick's answer was the belief that God has supplied us today with the resources needed to help out families who are experiencing a need. Long before "see a need, meet a need" became a popular phrase, it was part of Rick.

Rick and his wife, Joan, never had a lot of money but whatever they had was always readily available for whatever needs they noticed throughout the day.

A GENEROUS TWIST STORY

When Hurricane Andrew struck the south Florida coast back in 1992 a number of relief agencies showed up ready to work. Rick wasn't a part of any of them. He was simply a guy living in the Miami area who saw needs all around him and was willing to do anything to help. When the Red Cross and the Salvation Army set up command stations in the parking lot of First Baptist Church of Perrine they had large tents, multiple tables, and a lot of volunteers working together. Rick set up a card table in the parking lot next to them and simply started collecting people's names and addresses with notes on them as to what their needs might be.

Using the network of Youth For Christ programs across the United States, Rick began recruiting donations and volunteer laborers who were willing to give time and energy to helping people who had lost everything. From this humble beginning emerged a disaster relief ministry by the name of Project TeamWork. Rick's generosity was contagious. Through Project TeamWork, Rick oversaw the reconstruction of 1,000 homes utilizing more than 14,000 volunteers in Homestead and Florida City.

"Dear children, let's not merely say that we love each other; let us show the truth by our actions." 1 John 3.18 (NLT)

Rick lived this out every day, doing everything within his power to meet the needs of others. Rick embodied what it means to live a life that is truly Christ-like. And while Rick entered his eternal home back in May of 2004, the memory of how he lived his life lives on in the lives of people his life touched.

As I sit at my desk writing this, God is revealing to me once again that a world of needs surrounds me and I continue holding tightly on to what I have wrongly come to believe is mine. I am too caught up in my own needs and wants to help others. I wish someone would do something nice for me today. I want someone to buy me a cup of coffee or replace my broken snow blower. Reflecting on Rick's life reminds me that instead of focusing on my needs I need to realize that someone in my circle of friends needs a large coffee today.

Someone needs a new appliance. Someone simply needs a text letting them know that someone cares. And the truth is, living generously might mean changing my plans for today, it might mean changing my budget. It might mean going out of my way and heading back into the city.

You can begin to live generously today by simply buying a large cup of coffee for someone. That's what Rick would do.

34
DAY

ONLY
ONE THING

"We do not segment our lives, giving some time to God, some to our business or schooling, while keeping parts to ourselves. The idea is to live all of our lives in the presence of God, under the authority of God, and for the honor and glory of God. That is what the Christian life is all about." —R.C. Sproul

········ **DEVOTIONAL**

 Bible Passage

"As Jesus and the disciples continued on their way to Jerusalem, they came to a certain village where a woman named Martha welcomed him into her home. Her sister, Mary, sat at the Lord's feet, listening to what he taught. But Martha was distracted by the big dinner she was preparing. She came to Jesus and said, 'Lord, doesn't it seem unfair to you that my sister just sits here while I do all the work? Tell her to come and help me.' But the Lord said to her, 'My dear Martha, you are worried and upset over all these details! There is only one thing worth being concerned about. Mary has discovered it, and it will not be taken away from her.'"
Luke 10:38-42 (NLT)

 Questions

1. Reread the passage. Underline words and phrases that challenge us to live generously.

2. What is the "one thing" Jesus is talking about in this passage?

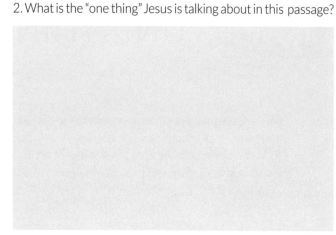

 ## Pray For

Others - Pastors you know, for renewal, strength, wisdom, and understanding of the "one thing".

Goodness - Let me not judge others, but instead see the goodness in those around me.

My Attitude - That I would live in the presence of God, under His authority and for His honor and glory.

 ## Today's Selfless Act

Send an encouraging note to your pastor and their family. If able, include a gift card.

Journal

Looking back on your day, describe how you met the challenge of generosity.

Journal

MY HELPER

Yesterday He helped me,
Today He did the same;
How long will this continue?
Forever! Praise His Name!
—Warren Wiersbe

 ## Bible Passage

"For the Lord your God is living among you.
He is a mighty savior.
He will take delight in you with gladness.
With his love, he will calm all your fears.
He will rejoice over you with joyful songs."
—Zephaniah 3:17 (NLT)

Questions

1. Reread the passage. Underline words and phrases that challenge us to live generously.

2. How has God calmed your past fears?

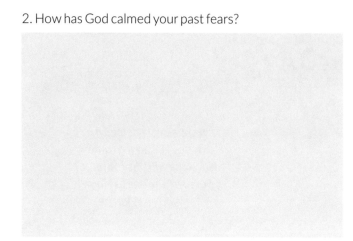

Pray For

Others - The World - that they may see God.

Joy - Help me to delight in You, Lord.

My Attitude - Pray for a willing heart, mind and soul to selflessly love, give, serve and live generously.

Today's Selfless Act

Spend 15 minutes alone with God today, outside if possible, listening to worship music. Let Him calm your fears and focus on His delight in you.

Journal

Looking back on your day, describe how you met the challenge of generosity.

Journal

TALK
ABOUT IT

"Most people who wind up in the kingdom of God can trace their salvation back to a single, life-changing conversation with a Christ-follower." —Bill Hybels

 Bible Passage

"But my life is worth nothing to me unless I use it for finishing the work assigned me by the Lord Jesus—the work of telling others the Good News about the wonderful grace of God." Acts 20:24 (NLT)

(?) **Questions**

1. Reread the passage. Underline words and phrases that challenge us to live generously.

2. What fears do you have about telling others about the Good News of God's grace?

Pray For

Others - My circle of influence to experience God today.

Faithful - Help me to live faithfully, trusting You and telling others about You.

My Attitude - Remove any fears and excuses that would keep me from telling others about Your wonderful grace, Lord.

Today's Selfless Act

Live out loud today! Tell someone today the Good News about the wonderful grace of God.

Journal

Looking back on your day, describe how you met the challenge of generosity.

Journal

LOVE ONE
ANOTHER

"I used to want to fix people, but now I just want to be with them." — Bob Goff

Bible Passage

"A new command I give you: Love one another. As I have loved you, so you must love one another. By this everyone will know that you are my disciples, if you love one another."
John 13:34-35 (NIV)

Questions

1. Reread the passage. Underline words and phrases that challenge us to live generously.

2. How is love defined in this passage?

 Pray For

Others - My circle of influence to experience God's love today.

Love - Help me to love people more than try to fix them.

My Attitude - Help my life to be judgment free so that I can generously love others.

 Today's Selfless Act

Be with someone today. No phones, no interruptions. Listen. Encourage. Love.

Journal

Looking back on your day, describe how you met the challenge of generosity.

Journal

DAY 38

PLANTING
SEEDS

"The only way to live a truly remarkable life is not to get everyone to notice you, but to leave noticeable marks of His love everywhere you go." —Ann Voskamp

········ DEVOTIONAL

Bible Passage

"Plant the good seeds of righteousness,
and you will harvest a crop of love.
Plow up the hard ground of your hearts,
for now is the time to seek the Lord,
that he may come
and shower righteousness upon you."
Hosea 10:12 (NLT)

Questions

1. Reread the passage. Underline words and phrases that challenge us to live generously.

2. What "crop" is growing from the seeds you have planted while living generously?

Pray For

Others - The elderly: their health, protection, finances, and families.

Self Control - Help me to be disciplined in the work You have prepared for me to accomplish.

My Attitude - Lord, give me the desire to work diligently without grumbling or complaining.

Today's Selfless Act

Buy a plant or some flowers for an elderly friend. If possible, deliver them in person.

Journal

Looking back on your day, describe how you met the challenge of generosity.

Journal

GIVE, GIVE, GIVE

"I cannot think of a better definition of Christianity than that: give, give, give." — James I. McCord

Bible Passage

"For this is how God loved the world: He gave his one and only Son, so that everyone who believes in him will not perish but have eternal life."
John 3:16 (NLT)

Questions

1. Reread the passage. Underline words and phrases that challenge us to live generously.

2. What have you learned about generous living?

Pray For

Others - The world - that they may know the love of God and believe in Him.

Love - Fill me with Your love so that I can love others.

My Attitude - Take away my selfish thoughts and help me to live selflessly, generously loving, giving, serving and living for You.

Today's Selfless Act

Write a letter to your pastor or someone who has positively influenced you in a spiritual way. Let them know the impact their ministry has had on your life.

Journal

Looking back on your day, describe how you met the challenge of generosity.

Journal

40 DAY

GLAD AND SINCERE HEARTS

"The sun looks down on nothing half so good as a household laughing together over a meal." — C. S. Lewis

 Bible Passage

"Everyone was filled with awe at the many wonders and signs performed by the apostles. All the believers were together and had everything in common. They sold property and possessions to give to anyone who had need. Every day they continued to meet together in the temple courts. They broke bread in their homes and ate together with glad and sincere hearts, praising God and enjoying the favor of all the people. And the Lord added to their number daily those who were being saved." Acts 2:43-47 (NIV)

 Questions

1. Reread the passage. Underline words and phrases that challenge us to live generously.

2. Why do you think it is important to gather people together in your home?

Pray For

Others - Friends to experience God's joy.

Joy - Fill my home with joy so that others will see You and give You praise.

My Attitude - May my life reflect the joy I have because I am Your child.

Today's Selfless Act

Plan a Pasta Dinner. Grab your calendar, pick a night this week and invite people over for dinner or dessert. Host a simple gathering (ask a friend to help)—pizza, pasta, hot dogs, ice cream sundaes, or take out. It doesn't have to be elaborate. Invite people you know well and others you don't know as well. Contact your guest list today.

Journal

Looking back on your day, describe how you met the challenge of generosity.

A Generous Twist Story
Investing In God's Kingdom

There's a young couple in their early 30s. They have 3 small children. The mom stays at home caring for the children and the dad works hard to provide for his family. They live a simple life in order to build their savings. They realize that a couple in their circle of influence, who have committed their lives to ministry, have a great need. So, after praying about it, they take the entire balance of $8,500.00 from their savings account and, in an extravagantly selfless move, generously give all to this ministry couple. Why? Because they understand the generous twist. They know it will be used to grow the Kingdom of God by this couple who have willingly put God's Kingdom before everything else.

CONGRATULATIONS!

Congratulations! You just completed the first leg of a path towards living the extravagantly selfless life that Jesus calls each of his followers to live. We are very excited that you've begun this journey and are grateful that we've been given the opportunity to walk down this path with you.

Recent studies show that it takes 66 days to form a habit in your life. Not that extravagant selflessness will ever become automatic for you, but you will notice that it will become easier and easier each day that you practice it. You have just completed the first 40 days on this journey, and it is our prayer that you would continue to faithfully walk this path for the next 26 days and beyond!

We encourage you over the next 26 days to read through the books of Philippians and James from the New Testament as you choose a daily activity from the list below or create your own list!

Take time today to reread your journal. Spend time thanking God for the opportunities He gave you to live with a generous twist. Were you able to notice changes in your own attitude about living an extravagantly selfless life like Jesus?

We would love to hear your stories. Share your Generous Twist stories online at facebook.com/generouschurchproject using #GenerousTwist. Feel free to email your stories to us at info@generouschurchproject.org.

MORE IDEAS

Individual Activities

Purchase a gift card at a store and give it to the person behind you in line

Take a meal to a senior citizen or a new mom and her family

Offer to babysit for free

Visit someone in an assisted living facility - weekly

Contact a prison ministry and get involved

Offer to watch someone's children while mom and dad clean the house or do a project

Open your home for Bible Study

Provide dinner for the staff at a local ministry

Help your neighbor.....fix their car, mow their lawn, shovel snow, power wash the house, plant flowers, clean out a closet

Memorize Bible verses with a friend

Wash your neighbor's car

Offer to put gas in the car of a widow or single parent

Individual Activities

Get a group together and do yard work for someone in need

Send weekly notes to someone in prison, or in an assisted living center

Visit someone in the hospital

Send a card to someone who is sick

Send a card to someone who is struggling

Send an encouraging/funny/thankful card to someone

Buy candy bars for everyone at work

Volunteer at a hospital

Volunteer in the Children's Ministry at your church

Organize a weekly/monthly dinner with neighbors, coworkers, or others

Purchase a gas card for a neighbor/friend

Empty your change jar and buy gift cards to send to college students or friends in need

Group Activities

Sing at an assisted living facility or retirement village

Organize a work day to help widows in your church

Make cookies and deliver to individuals who are home-bound

Serve at a soup kitchen—make it a monthly event

Prepare goodie bags for homeless folks

Host a babysitting night so parents can have a night off

Conduct a food drive for a local food bank

Volunteer to play games, puzzles, or music at a retirement community

Host an ice cream party for your neighborhood and have everyone bring toppings to share